ANIMALS IN THE CITY

# Deer

**Ava Podmorow**

Explore other books at:
WWW.ENGAGEBOOKS.COM

VANCOUVER, B.C.

e WWW.ENGAGEBOOKS.COM

*Deer: Level Pre-1*
*Animals in the City*
Podmorow, Ava  2004 –
Text © 2022 Engage Books
Design © 2022 Engage Books

Edited by: A.R. Roumanis
and Sarah Harvey

Text set in Epilogue

FIRST EDITION / FIRST PRINTING

LIBRARY AND ARCHIVES CANADA CATALOGUING IN PUBLICATION

Title: Deer / Ava Podmorow.
Names: Podmorow, Ava, author.
Description: Series statement: Animals in the city
Engaging readers: level pre-1, beginner.

Identifiers: Canadiana (print) 20220398682 | Canadiana (ebook) 20220398690
ISBN 978-1-77476-740-5 (hardcover)
ISBN 978-1-77476-741-2 (softcover)
ISBN 978-1-77476-742-9 (epub)
ISBN 978-1-77476-743-6 (pdf)

Subjects:
LCSH: Readers (Elementary)
LCSH: Readers—Deer.
LCGFT: Readers (Publications)

Classification: LCC PE1119.2 .P633 2022 | DDC J428.6/2—DC23

This project has been made possible in part
by the Government of Canada.                    Canada

Did you see
that deer?

Deer come to cities from wild areas nearby.

They are looking
for food.

A male deer is
called a buck.

A female deer is called a doe.

Does have babies in the spring.

**Spots**

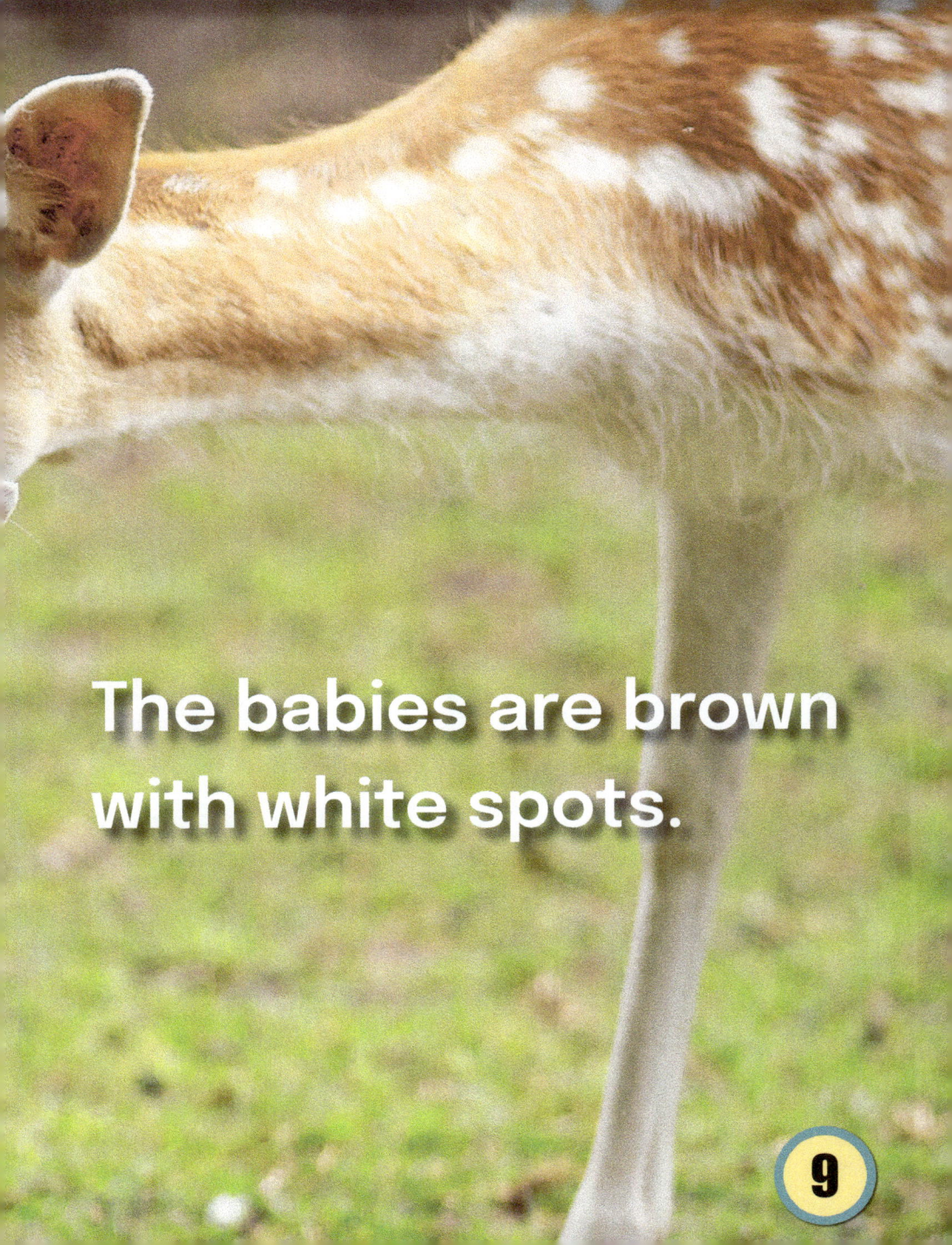

The babies are brown with white spots.

Baby deer are called fawns.

They stay very close to their mothers.

**Antlers**

Male deer grow antlers every year.

Antlers fall off
in the winter.

A group of deer
is called a herd.

15

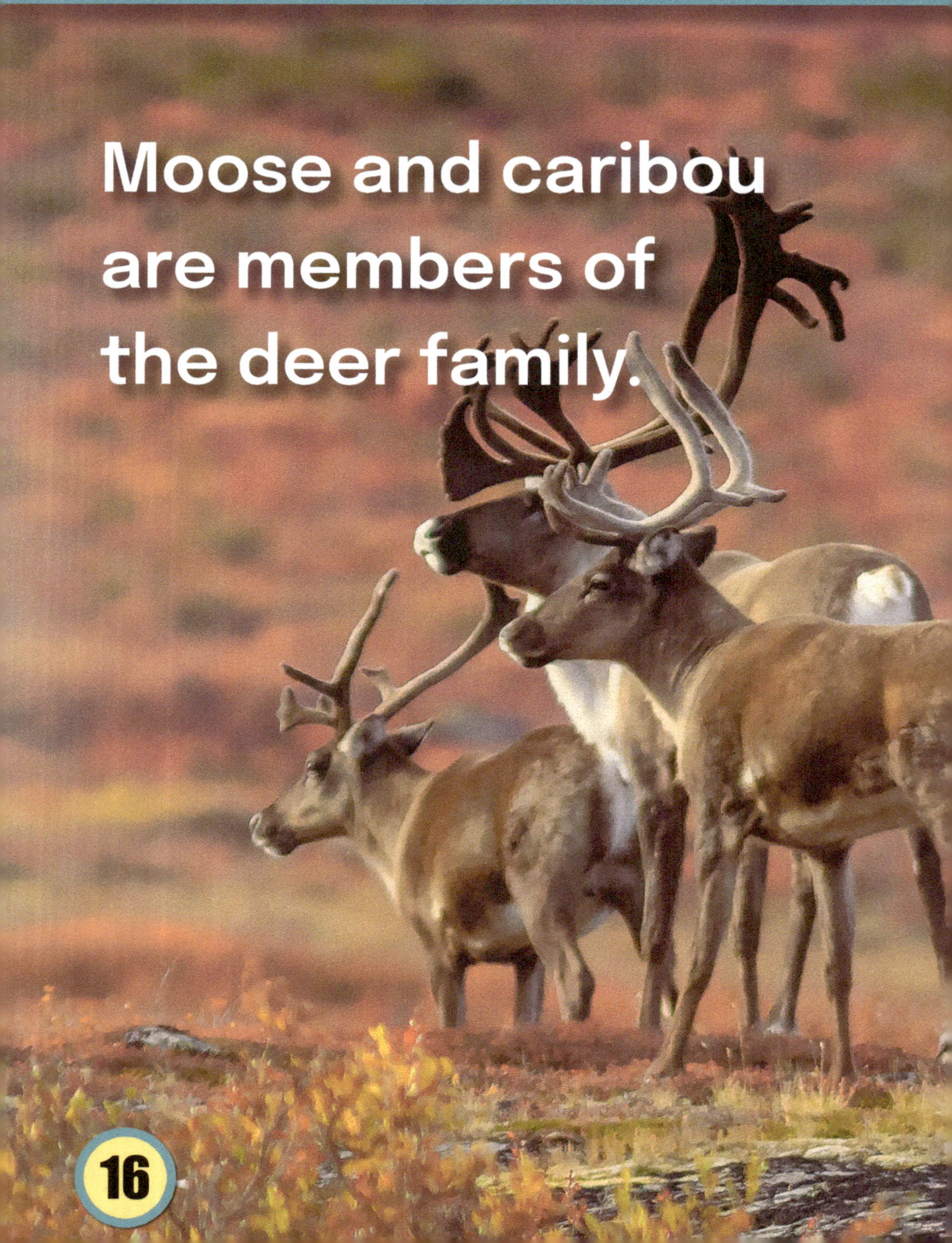

Moose and caribou are members of the deer family.

**Caribou**

There are over 60 kinds of deer.

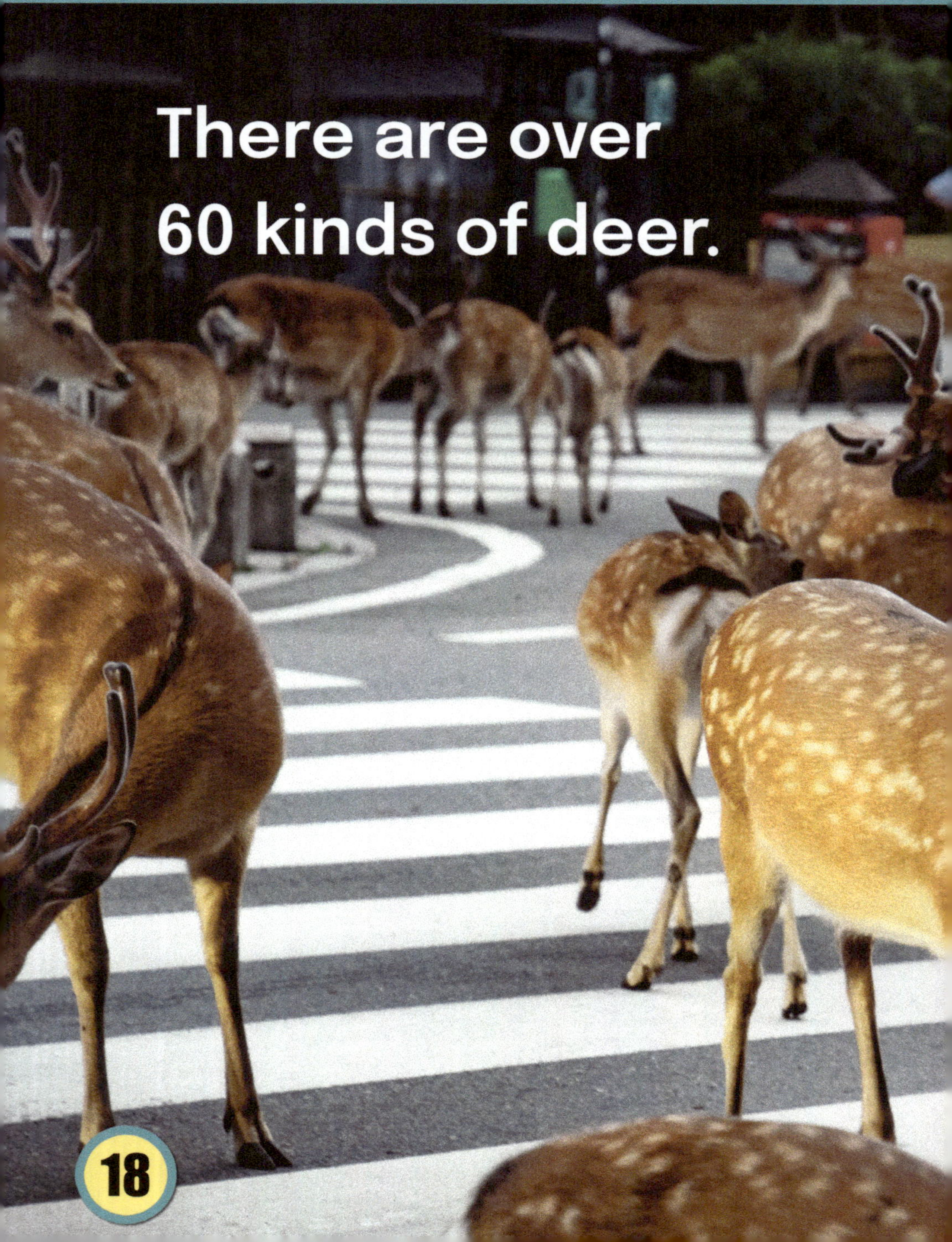

Sika deer

**Deer can run very fast!**

They can not
run for very
long though.

# Deer are really good swimmers!

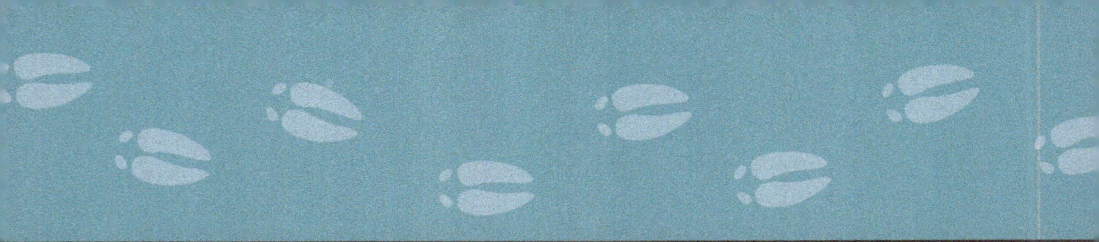

23

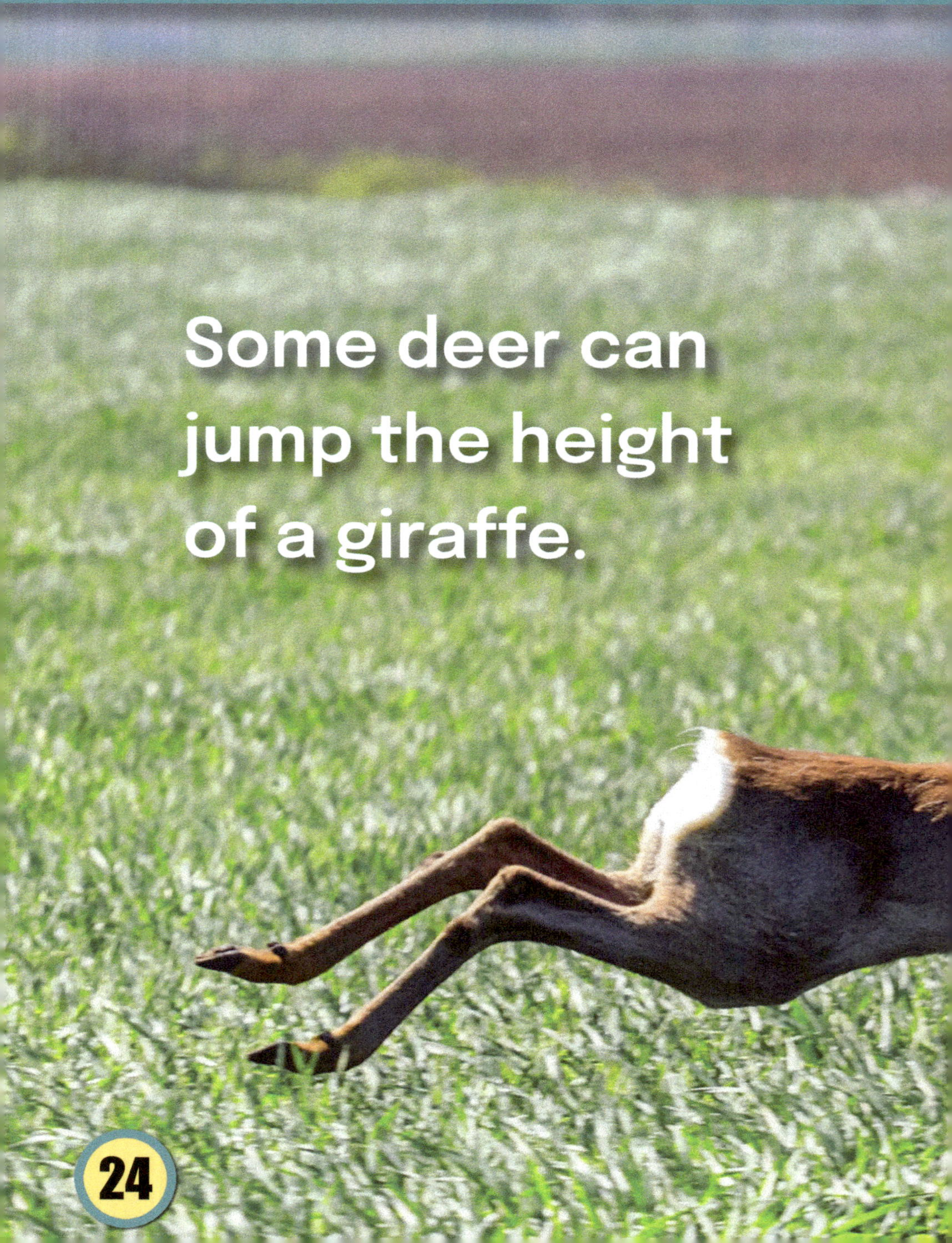

Some deer can jump the height of a giraffe.

Roe deer

Deer have a good
sense of smell
and hearing.

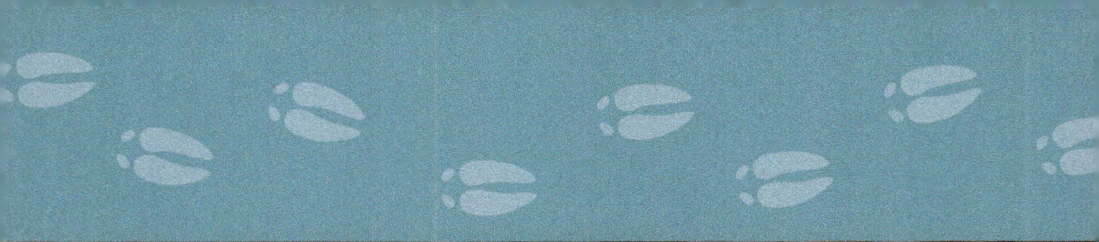

They can not
see very well.

Thank you for sharing your garden with me!

29

# Explore other books in the Animals In The City series.

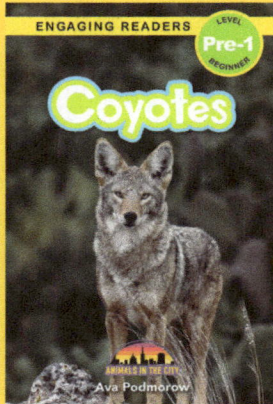

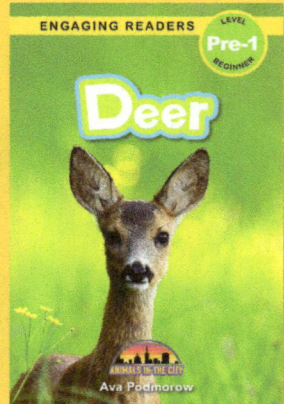

ENGAGING READERS — LEVEL Pre-1 BEGINNER — **Cats** — ANIMALS IN THE CITY — Ava Podmorow

ENGAGING READERS — LEVEL Pre-1 BEGINNER — **Coyotes** — ANIMALS IN THE CITY — Ava Podmorow

ENGAGING READERS — LEVEL Pre-1 BEGINNER — **Deer** — ANIMALS IN THE CITY — Ava Podmorow

ENGAGING READERS — LEVEL Pre-1 BEGINNER — **Owls** — ANIMALS IN THE CITY — Ava Podmorow

ENGAGING READERS — LEVEL Pre-1 BEGINNER — **Pigeons** — ANIMALS IN THE CITY — Ava Podmorow

ENGAGING READERS — LEVEL Pre-1 BEGINNER — **Rabbits** — ANIMALS IN THE CITY — Ava Podmorow

ENGAGING READERS — LEVEL Pre-1 BEGINNER — **Raccoons** — ANIMALS IN THE CITY — Sarah Harvey

ENGAGING READERS — LEVEL Pre-1 BEGINNER — **Rats** — ANIMALS IN THE CITY — Ava Podmorow

ENGAGING READERS — LEVEL Pre-1 BEGINNER — **Skunks** — ANIMALS IN THE CITY — Ava Podmorow

Visit www.engagebooks.com/readers

# Explore level 1 readers with the Animals That Make a Difference series.

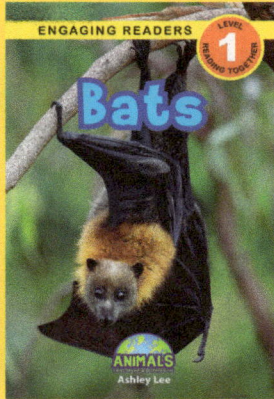

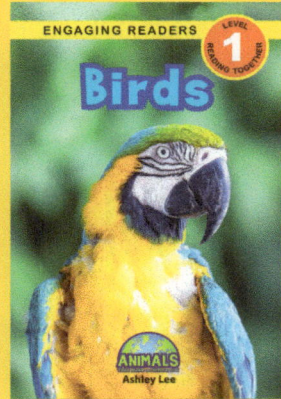

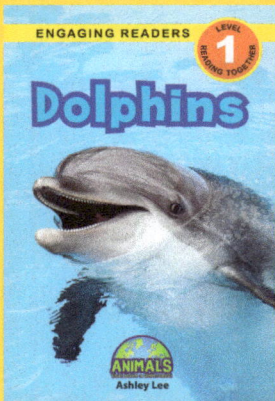

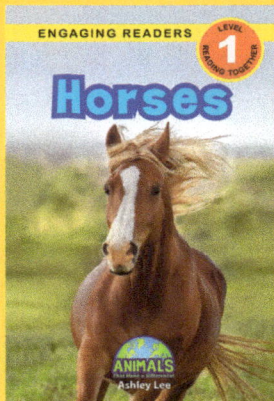

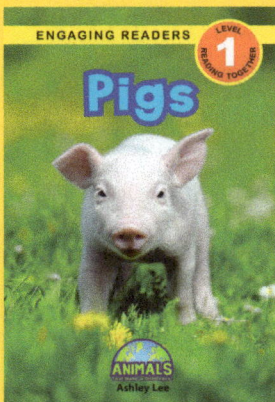

Visit www.engagebooks.com/readers

www.ingramcontent.com/pod-product-compliance
Lightning Source LLC
Chambersburg PA
CBHW051235020426
42331CB00016B/3391